A life

Verity Boxall

BookLeaf
Publishing

Presentation by *BookLeaf Publishing*

Web: www.bookleafpub.com

E-mail: info@bookleafpub.com

ISBN: 9789357697262

First edition 2023

DEDICATION

For my Mum, now and always.

ACKNOWLEDGEMENT

Life is short. Enjoy it whilst you can. Learn to dance in the rain.

PREFACE

Appreciate what you have, you never know
when it might disappear.

Dinner dance

She wore a purple ball gown,
Hair clips sparkled in the candlelight,
Her face was radiant beauty,
The room was filled with her infectious laughter,
Waist length black hair fell straight down,
A smile that captured your heart,
Her slim figure was the envy of many,
The scent of her perfume lingered in your mind,
She wore a purple ball gown.

The most powerful emotion

Madness and despair,
Dejection or elation,
Courage, strength and hope.

Daffodil field

The daffodils call to me
Their bright colours herald Spring.
On that morning walk they called to her-
Wordsworth sprung forth.
Would that we have daffodils for all time.

Pea souper

Where have you gone?
Would that I could follow but I lost you in the fog.
I ran after your shadow but it was a deception.
Desperately, I struck matches to lead you back to the light,
But the wind blew fiercely and I could not protect the path.
Still I stand, howling your name into the night.

Australia

She was there and
Then she was not,
A perplexed four year old and
A voice calling from the depths,
"blasted manhole."

Youth

Hum me a lullaby,
Scratch my back,
Hold me close,
Everything will be alright.

Follow my directions

It's this way she said
And we believed her.
Just like the last time
And the one before
That.
"Life is an adventure!"
She said.
So how do we get out of this field of sheep in
our car?
Again?

How deep is your love?

This is the song they danced to
On their wedding day,
They have lived hand in glove
For over forty years,
Always keeping the rhythm of their own harmonious beat,
Now the music fractures and someone is out of step,
The other valiantly tries to adjust to the new moves,
The song comes on again, asking its question.
The answer is; never ending.

The Blue Book

The heat was enough to melt the soul but it
settled for the ones on my shoes,
Our clothes were drenched in sweat as we
climbed the hill to see . . .
A crumbling white wall with bullet holes
Ozymandius struck again
"Splash!" was the noise we made as we jumped
in the village fountain.

Wish for an old-fashioned egg timer

The sand is rapidly slipping away
The invisible current sure and strong
Her memories are beginning to fray

Glimpses of sunlight, she so wants to stay
But the waves rush in and pull her along
The sand is rapidly slipping away

On the beach, she moves and begins to sway
But one misstep and she forgets the song
Her memories are beginning to fray

Come with me into the salty, sea spray
But she's scared and feels she doesn't belong
The sand is rapidly slipping away

Let's build sandcastles, what games we can play
But she gets cross when she gets it all wrong
Her memories are beginning to fray

O nature! I cry. Why must you decay?
I want her to stay and time to prolong
The sand is rapidly slipping away
Her memories are beginning to fray

Drainpipe drama

There once was a little 'to do.'
Re a payment when notes were too few.
So she threw down a cheque
And straight done the neck
Of the drainpipe it went.
Toodle oo!

Memories

You held my hand when I was small,
You dried my tears when I did fall,
I learnt lots of history,
As I was sat on your knee,
Your food was simply the best,
It always outshone the rest,
To music, you danced away,
Lots of fun and games to play,
Your laughter was always there,
I knew I was in your care,
Now you are always in mine.

Bluebells

Gently bobbing in the breeze
Their blue creates a carpet of ocean
To walk upon.
They give off an ethereal perfume that quickly fades,
A wild flower, not around for long but beautiful when
in bloom,
These are her favourite and I love taking her to see
them in the woods,
Even if she forgets their name.

Losing words

People can put things in odd places when they get older,
Either objects, their memory or both.
They put keys in the fridge or forget they have glasses on
their head.
Sometimes though, the places can get odder like
toothbrushes in bedside drawers and deodorant in a sock.
The trick is knowing when to laugh and when to cry. How
to try to accept the unacceptable.
Sometimes people can get lost inside their minds and their
memories get jumbled up like laundry in a washing
machine.
You know, where you end up missing a sock when the wash
is done but you're sure you put it in.
It's like that with memories sometimes, something is there
but it's out of reach and can't be grasped.

Her love is still there

If there's anything you need then let me know.
…
If there's anything you need then let me know.
…
If there's anything you need then let me know.
…
If there's anything you need then let me know.
…
If there's anything you need then let me know.

Working life

Clack, clack, clack, ding
Went the old-fashioned typewriter of her youth,
Clack, clack, clack ding
As she zoomed through her work.
Clack, clack, clack, ding
She had an excellent typing speed.
Clack, clack, clack, ding
The secretary who was always in demand.
Clack, clack, clack, ding

Upon a star

Sometimes I go driving with the music blaring,
Sometimes I go out into the cold, night air craving
stillness,
Sometimes I cry as I drive home,
Sometimes I laugh hysterically,
Sometimes this disease takes my breath away,
Sometimes you're there, actually present with me,
Sometimes I am left to imagine you as you were,
Sometimes I talk to a younger memory of you,
Sometimes I ask this memory for advice,
Sometimes I imagine what you would say to me,
Sometimes we dance together in my mind,
Sometimes I imagine we explore art galleries
together, like we used to do,
Sometimes I wish, I just wish. . .

Portrait

You and I,
Me and you,
You always were the prettier one.
Pixie features,
Petite frame,
I took after Dad.
Except my eyes, my nose and my sense of
humour.
These are utterly you.
You and I,
Me and you.

Ingram Content Group UK Ltd.
Milton Keynes UK
UKHW021008130623
423366UK00015B/463

9 789357 697262